JOB INTERVIEWS
Made Easy

JOB INTERVIEWS
Made Easy

Patty Marler　　Jan Bailey Mattia

VGM Career Horizons
NTC/Contemporary Publishing Group

DEDICATION

Jeff-

Your love, support, and belief in me have given me the
encouragement I needed to try… and to be the best I can be.

-Patty

Gerry-

For planting the seed and challenging me to push the limits.

-Jan

Library of Congress Cataloging-in-Publication Data

Marler, Patty.
    Job interviews made easy / by Patty Marler, Jan Bailey Mattia.
       p.   cm.
    ISBN 0-8442-4349-3
    1. Employment interviewing.   I. Mattia, Jan Bailey.   II. Title.
HF5549.5.I6M316   1995
650.14—dc20   95-775
                                      CIP

Published by VGM Career Books
A division of NTC/Contemporary Publishing Group, Inc.
4255 West Touhy Avenue, Lincolnwood (Chicago), Illinois 60712-1975 U.S.A.
Copyright © 1995 by NTC/Contemporary Publishing Group, Inc.
Printed in the United States of America
International Standard Book Number: 0-8442-4349-3

00 01 02 03 04 05 VP 22 21 20 19 18 17 16 15 14 13 12 11 10 9 8 7 6

Contents

CHAPTER 2: BECOMING AN ACTIVE PARTICIPANT   22

CHAPTER 3: THE INTERVIEW   33

Introduction

The job interview can be one of the most nerve–racking, anxiety–ridden events you will ever experience. Few other experiences have such a drastic impact on the direction your life will take, yet we often fail to plan and prepare for the job interview as we should. By being both ready and informed you will get a handle on your career path.

Job Interviews Made Easy will guide you through the job interview and show you how to make the most of your opportunities.

 "Today is just the beginning."
– Jim Williams

Interview Scenarios appear at the beginning and end of the book; they look at two people's job interviews, how each person prepared and what results they got. They provide valuable information on what each person did well and what could be improved, and they will be useful in helping you analyze your strengths and weaknesses in interview situations.

We also identify **Interview Varieties** and outline their format and purpose. Then we give you tips on **Becoming an Active Participant** in the interview process—how to sell yourself and your skills effectively. **The Interview** and the course it runs are outlined with sample questions and responses. **Follow Up,** a necessity in today's job market, is laid out so you can be sure to secure that job.

Changes in today's approach to the job interview are reviewed in the **That Was Then . . . This Is Now** section. **You're Offered the Job, Now What?** outlines how to negotiate your salary, formalize the job offer, and finally start working.

 "Life is a journey, not a destination."

– Dr. Robert Anthony, _Think On_

Read, learn, and enjoy and you will be on the road to a successful job interview.

Special Features

Special elements throughout this book will help you pick out key points and apply your new knowledge.

 Notes clarify text with concise explanations.

 Helpful Hints make you stand out in the crowd of job seekers.

 Expansion Exercises make your performance more polished.

 Horror Stories are true tales about things you will want to avoid.

 **Director's Cuts** provide a running commentary on the job–seeker's performance throughout the interview.

 Special Thoughts will inspire and motivate you.

*Prepare, prepare, prepare and you **will** land that next job!!*

Interview Scenario 1: A Look at One Job Interview

Sarah has had a stable lifestyle and career in a small town. But a lot has happened recently, so much that everything seems like a blur. Her husband passed away suddenly last year and her youngest daughter moved away to college in the fall, leaving her alone. Sarah thinks it would be nice to live in a larger city and now is the perfect time to make the move.

Sarah knows if she moves she will have a hard time finding a job as good as the bank manager's position she now holds, but she's tired of the work. She has been in the profession for nearly 20 years and the spark is no longer there; at this point in her life, Sarah needs 'spark' from somewhere. A career change is what she needs and insurance adjusting is where she feels she can regain vitality and excitement in her life. The decision made, Sarah signs up for the one–year adjusting program at the same college her daughter is attending. Sarah is moving on and today is the first day of the rest of her life.

"Choose a job you love and you'll never have to work a day in your life."

Confucius

The year in college flies by and graduation day is quickly approaching. The next step is to find a job. Sarah knew it would be difficult locating an adjustor's position with her recent training in the area, her age, and the tight job market, but Sarah never thought it would be this difficult. A resume service compiled her resume and, although she thought there was little substance to it, it looked very nice. Who was she to question what should be in a resume? They are the professionals. Sarah mails 15 resumes to companies who have advertised positions, but she doesn't get a single call for an interview. She is beginning to feel frustrated and worried.

Sarah has met a few people in the industry over the past year, but she has not wanted to involve them in her job search; they are friends, and she doesn't want to pressure them. It is getting to the point, however, where she is beginning to feel desperate; she needs work. Finally she begins meeting with friends and discussing her career aspirations and within two weeks she hears about a position and is asked to submit her resume. Sarah hand–delivers it this time and desperately hopes for an interview. She receives a telephone call two days later and is asked to meet the vice–president.

 Be sure you have the final say about your resume. The final product must be a reflection of you, not someone else's idea of you.

Sarah has not been interviewed for 10 years and, although she has conducted interviews at the bank, she still feels nervous and afraid. The meeting is scheduled at the main branch of an international insurance company and there are 11 candidates for the job. Sarah is concerned about the competition, and isn't sure how to prepare. Reviewing the questions she normally asked when she conducted interviews seems like a good start and after 20 minutes she feels ready . . . nervous, but ready.

 Choose two outfits before the interview. Make sure they are clean and pressed and appropriate for the type of work you are applying for. Conservative is best.

The day of the interview Sarah chooses a conservative but attractive business suit. Everything is going as scheduled until she spills her coffee onto her blazer. What a mess!! Now what is she going to wear?! Frantically she runs to the closet to decide on another outfit, never an easy task for Sarah. Finally, she chooses an outfit which is not as appropriate, but will have to do. "Rats." Now she is flustered and feeling frenzied, not what she needs at this point.

Already ten minutes behind schedule, Sarah grabs her purse and car keys and runs out the door. She isn't familiar with the area of the city where her interview will be and needs time to find the building. Oh well, she remembered to put the address in her purse the night before and the drive will give her time to relax.

Allow 30 minutes extra the day of the interview. It is better to be early than late!

Finding the building turns out to be easier than anticipated, but parking is a problem. The downtown core has limited parking; the closest is four blocks away. Sarah has to run to make up time and is panting and perspiring when she arrives. Oh, things are not going well so far and the feeling of panic is starting to intensify.

Do a 'test run' the day before the interview to be sure you know where the building is, how long it takes to get there, and where to park.

After a quick stop in the washroom, Sarah calms down, wipes the sweat off her brow, and regains some composure before entering the office.

Wonderful! It's better to take one minute in the washroom before the interview than to discover lettuce from lunch in your teeth afterward.

Luckily, the previous interviews have run slightly over and Sarah has more time to catch her breath and collect herself. The receptionist asks if she would like coffee and Sarah gracefully declines, remembering the morning coffee incident, but asks for a glass of water to take the dry sensation from her mouth. Sarah appreciates how pleasant the receptionist is and notices how happy all the employees who walk by appear to be. This looks like a place where she would like to work.

 Good work. Keep your eyes and ears open at all times. You never know when you will hear something you can mention in the interview or that will help you decide if you want to work for the company.

"Sarah, they will see you now. Please follow me and I'll take you to the conference room."

Conference room! Sarah isn't prepared for more than one person interviewing her! She thought she was meeting with the vice–president of the company only, but there appears to be more involved than that. Sarah tries to relax and convince herself there is nothing she can do now.

 Find out how many people will be involved before the interview. Try to remember the names and titles of the interviewers.

The receptionist opens the door of the conference room and there are three people waiting inside. "Sarah," she begins, "this is Jesse White, the vice–president of our company, Cory Bouchant, director of Adjusting, and Bobby Marr, supervisor of the Northwest Adjusting Division."

Three people, Sarah thinks, Help!

"Hello, I am pleased to meet you," Sarah responds with a slight crack in her voice.

Sarah sits down quickly, hoping they won't see her shaking. She forgot to shake hands, but decides her hands were too sweaty anyway.

Discreetly wipe your hand on your slacks or skirt just before shaking hands. No one will ever know you have sweaty palms!

"It is nice to meet you, Sarah," begins Jesse. "I hope you didn't have trouble finding the office."

"No," Sarah says.

 Stop! Never answer with a simple 'Yes' or 'No'; this says nothing about you, is boring to listen to, and makes the interview go by too quickly. Take a relaxed approach by elaborating and saying more about yourself. You will seem more like a real person, and full answers lead to more questions.

"Terri told us you recently moved," Jesse says. Why, after living so long in a small town, would you decide to move to a large city?"

"My husband passed away two years ago and my children have relocated to various cities to go to school, so I had no family left in my home town. The chance of my children returning was remote, so I decided if I wanted to be close to them, I was the one who would have to move. I chose this city because my daughter lives here, and it is clean and safe. I also wanted to return to school and discovered there was an excellent adjustor's course available at the local college. I'm having fun getting to know new people and making new friends, and am very happy with my decision to move."

 **Good for you! That is a much better answer than 'because' or 'to go to school.'**

Bobby leans over and takes the copy of Sarah's resume from Jesse. "I see you were a bank manager. Why did you become involved in insurance adjusting?"

"I thought it would be interesting and exciting and I would have the opportunity to meet new people." What else, what else, Sarah thinks. She can't think of anything else, so she hopes that answer will do.

 Now is a good time to talk about your 'transferable skills' . . . those skills you used before, which can be used in your new occupation or job.

"Tell us what you know about our company," Cory suggests.

Sarah begins to perspire again. She hasn't thought to do any research on the company. She knows everything about the banking industry and forgot that she doesn't know much about the companies involved in insurance. Think Sarah, THINK!

"Actually, um, I don't know very much at all about your company."

 Oh no, even if you didn't do any research, you can still say more based on general knowledge of the industry or what you saw in the waiting room. Always indicate your enthusiasm to learn more about the company.

"We have a very good reputation and customer satisfaction is very important to us," replies Jesse. "Sometimes, however, our adjustors have a difficult time maintaining that positive company image, such as when they must reject a customer's claim or tell them they will receive less money than they anticipated. As an adjustor, how would you make sure the customer is left feeling satisfied under these conditions?"

"Honesty is the best policy," Sarah answers. "It's important to be straightforward with customers so they know what they are dealing with. I would assess the situation and if I thought the person was expecting more money than we could pay, I'd tell them I need to review the situation. Then I would write them a letter explaining why they aren't entitled to what they thought."

"Why wouldn't you tell them in person?"

"I feel I can better explain myself in writing and am able to maintain better control of the situation that way. I don't like when customers are angry and I feel flustered when it happens. I find a letter works well and if the customer insists on more explanation, I can explain it over the phone. I find this is the best way to avoid confrontations and conflicts."

 You started nicely but blew it at the end—your fear of confrontation is obvious. Practice dealing with people's concerns in a direct way, and tell the employer this is a skill you are working on.

There is a pause, the panel seems surprised. Cory finally looks at the interview sheet and asks, "Sometimes our adjustors must work very long hours over several weeks or months. How do you feel about working long hours?"

Sarah is uncomfortable with this question and unconsciously begins clicking her pen. "This is not something I want at this point in my life. How often would you expect me to work long hours?"

 Ask friends and family what your nervous habits are. Make a point of watching for them during an interview.

"Well, it is very unpredictable," begins Cory. "Unexpected storms, crime, or a temporary decrease in staff would mean longer hours which could last one month of a year or even, on rare occasions, five months. We can't predict, but we do expect our adjustors to be flexible when we need them."

"Well, if it was expected, I would be willing to work the hours," Sarah replies hesitantly. She needs the job, and feels she can put up with these conditions until she can convince them to hire more people or she finds something else. "How would I be compensated financially for these extra hours?"

You didn't convince them! And it's a little early in the interview to be discussing salary. Save this question until nearer the end.

"We have a very fair compensation package we can discuss at a later date."

Sarah wonders, "Would I be able to take time off in lieu of time worked?"

Jesse takes control of the response to this question. "Due to the structure of our adjusting department, it would be highly unlikely. Under special circumstances, we might be able to consider it, but not normally."

There is an uncomfortable pause before Sarah is asked the next question. "What skills and qualifications do you possess that would make you a good insurance adjustor?"

"Well, I did outline them in my resume, but I can go over them again. I have the education you require, but I don't have any experience in the adjusting field. I would really like the job, though, and am sure I would do well."

First, never assume the employer remembers what is in your resume. They may have read 200 and may be interviewing 11 people; they cannot keep everyone straight. Second, you implied you have no skills to be an adjustor, Discuss your transferable skills and emphasize past experience.

"What are your career aspirations; where do you hope to be in five years?"

Sarah is prepared for this question; it's one of the questions she asked all the people she interviewed. She gives a clear concise response that would please any employer looking for someone willing to commit themselves to the company.

The remainder of the interview continues on much the same tone. When the panel is through asking questions, they ask Sarah if she has any.

"Well, I do have one. I was told you were interviewing for two positions. Which one are you interviewing me for?"

 **You should have asked this question at the beginning of the interview, not the end. It appears you will accept any position offered and, while this may be true, you want to appear to have a specific career goal.**

Bobby explains what the position entails and describes a typical day. "Anything else?"

"No, I think you have answered all my questions. I just want to say how much I would like to work for your company. I know I do not have any experience as an adjustor, but I am sure you would be pleased with my work. I have brought a list of references and if you call them, they will vouch for my dedication and hard work."

 **Nice closing remarks. You showed your interest and highlighted two strong personal traits . . . dedication and hard work.**

The four of them say their goodbyes and this time Sarah remembers to shake everyone's hand. On her way out she takes the time to make small talk with the receptionist and asks for some information on the company's insurance policies.

 You should have collected this material before the interview, but better late than never. You may be able to use it in your thank you note.

Sarah leaves feeling good about the interview, but isn't sure how she came across. She'll just have to wait until they call to find out. She wonders how long that will be.

 Before you leave the interview, ask when you may call to find out if a decision has been made. Call back on the suggested date.

A week later Sarah receives a telephone call from Jesse. They've filled the position and unfortunately Sarah was not the candidate chosen.

Jesse wishes Sarah luck in her job search and thanks her for taking the time to attend the interview. Her resume will be kept on file for six months and be reviewed should any further positions become available. Sarah is disappointed but remembers to thank Jesse before hanging up.

Sarah had hoped to land this position. At least she has been through her first interview and feels she will be better prepared for the next one. She continues her job search.

 Ask for feedback after an interview, whether you're offered a job or not. DO NOT make the same mistakes twice!

Chapter 1

Interview Varieties

You are about to begin your journey into the world of job interviews and discover ideas that didn't exist in the interview world 20 years ago. No longer is there one standard job interview; employers use various strategies and techniques to determine who is the right person for the job. It is important to be prepared for anything and everything a potential employer can throw at you.

Jump in, hang on, discover, and learn!

"You must give up the way it is . . .
to have it the way you want it."

Dr. Robert Anthony, *Think On*

Interview Progression

"Success is that old ABC—ability,
breaks, and courage."

Charles Luckman

Employers often find it necessary to interview candidates more than once before a suitable person is chosen. You may experience only one or as many as five interviews for a position before the employer makes a final decision.

Preliminary Interviews

Preliminary interviews are the first interviews you attend and are designed to screen out unsuitable candidates. There is usually a large pool of 10–15 candidates who have been selected by the employer through reviewing resumes; speaking informally with job seekers; and taking referrals from other employers, friends, coworkers, or employment agencies.

The primary purpose of the preliminary interview is to give the employer a chance to become familiar with the candidates.

(For more information, see **Types of Interviews**).

 Ask how many people the employer will be interviewing. This may give you an idea of how many different sets and types of interviews will be conducted.

How?

Employers usually ask general questions regarding:

- knowledge and education

- personal reactions to various situations

- past experience and behavior

- who you are and what you like to do

    This is the time to create a great first impression!

What?

Employers select applicants who qualify for second interviews on the basis of information gathered in the preliminary interview.

- A new understanding of a person's experience

- The number of 'correct' responses to questions

- Candidates' overall responses to questions
- A general 'feel' for the person and whether they will fit in with the company and its philosophies.

Remember:

Employers take into consideration everything—from your responses and attitude to your dress and the confidence you project.

The more interviews you attend, the more focused the questions will become to the position.

There may be as many as three preliminary interviews before employers feel comfortable moving on to the selection interview. Be patient and give your all for each interview!

Selection Interviews

The goal of the selection interview is to make a final hiring decision. Employers already have a good 'feel' for the applicants and are now able to narrow the field further and make a final decision.

Prior to the selection interview, employers may have conducted one or more preliminary interviews and feel they are close to a final hiring decision. This is your last chance to impress the employer with your skills, personality, and flair!

"Forget your past track record.
Each moment is a new beginning."

Dr. Robert Anthony, *Think On*

During selection interviews employers:

- ask questions directly related to the job
- want to know how candidates would handle specific job situations, often asking job scenario questions.
- try to discover how each candidate would 'fit' with the other employees in their department
- evaluate drive, eagerness, and initiative

There are usually no more than two selection interviews, and only two or three candidates. If you make it this far, you are doing very well.

Combination Interviews

Because of time and/or budget restraints, some employers choose to combine preliminary and selection interviews into one extended interview. This type of interview can be long and gruelling and *all* questions the interviewer wants answered will be asked.

 **There was a young lad from Carruther
Who to an interview did bring his mother
Well she talked the whole way,
"For my son" she would say,
And the job? Well, it went to another.**

Sell yourself! It's your responsibility to be sure the employer knows everything necessary to hire you.

ypes of Interviews

As competition for jobs increases, it has become more and more common for human resources managers and all hiring personnel to implement a number of screening methods to make their job less time–consuming and more efficient. The result has been an increase in the screening practices used before interviewing candidates in person.

"If you wish in this world to advance, Your merits you're bound to enhance; You must stir it up and stump it, And blow your own trumpet. Or, trust me, you haven't a chance."

–W.S.Gilbert

Telephone Interviews

Telephone screening interviews are becoming more common and more popular. Take the time to practice telephone interviews with a friend. Be sure to make it as realistic as possible, ie: questions, dress, energy level, etc.

Telephone interviews are becoming more popular as the modern career market becomes global. People from distant cities and even distant countries are applying for positions and the telephone is an efficient way to 'meet' candidates prior to a personal interview. In unusual cases an individual may even be hired on the basis of a telephone interview.

Treat the telephone interview as you would any interview. It's hard to sound professional in your bathrobe and slippers.

Tip List

- Be organized. Clear an area by the telephone so you are not shuffling through papers during the interview.

- Have a pen and paper by the telephone.

- Have your list of questions handy.

- Have your resume and responses to tough questions ready to refer to.

- Do not eat, drink or smoke during the interview. No matter how careful you are, the employer knows you are distracted. What is more important, your lunch or the interview?

- Create a list of your most relevant skills and achievements so you remember to discuss them.

- Keep your voice **positive** and **energetic** and your answers **concise** and **easy to follow.** Your energy must come through in your voice and responses—interviewers cannot see your expressions!

 Telephone interviews are like an open book exam. You have all your notes right there, so be sure to use them!!

Computer Screening Interviews

 Use your job–hunt time constructively. When financially possible, take relevant courses or a good computer course. Continuing your education is great for your self esteem, your resume and building your network!

More and more, people are expected to be at least somewhat computer literate. This is frequently reflected in the hiring process. A screening interview becomes very time efficient when all that is required is a computer and some predetermined questions on a computer disc. Using this technique a company can evaluate your computer skills as well as have you answer job related questions to determine your eligibility for a position.

If you have no computer experience, make an introductory course a priority so that you become familiar and comfortable using computers.

 Go to a computer screening dressed as you would for a personal interview. You will feel more professional and confident and impress the boss if he or she drops in.

Tip List

- Take the time to refamiliarize yourself with the keyboard and computer.

- Type or write out your responses to potential questions as practice and so you are able to formalize your responses.

- Prepare an outline of information you want to highlight in your responses.

 You don't have to run out and buy a computer in order to participate in one of these screening interviews. Normally you will be asked to go to the personnel office so they can be sure it is indeed you answering the questions!

Questionnaires

Although a questionnaire is not normally considered an interview, many companies use written question and answer tests as a method of hiring employees. Questionnaires are used to determine the extent of your industry knowledge and may be given as a preliminary screening tool or as a final evaluation before hiring. Some industries use written tests more than others, such as for sales and market positions in insurance, automobiles, and pharmaceutics, or in technical occupations where specific knowledge is necessary.

 The more work you do in advance the more confident you will feel during your interview.

Tip List

- Know what skills the position requires.

- Review important aspects of your training and prepare to answer skill–testing questions.

- Complete a sample test at home, especially if it has been a while since you have been through a formal exam.

Video Tape Interviews

Video tape is not a common screening tool, but is used for some positions, typically where stress and quick reaction time are daily factors on the job. A video tape is made of situations, often stress–filled, that could occur in the position you are applying for. You watch the scenario on tape and answer questions as to how you would react in that situation. Again, this is often a screening tool. If your answers are suitable, you will be selected to progress in the competition.

Tip List

- Try to think of a similar situation you were involved in and use that as the basis for your answer.

- Be sure to highlight your strengths in your responses. It is easy to forget this when watching a video of someone else. Remember to illustrate how you would use **YOUR** skills and abilities in each situation.

- Look professional.

Personal Interviews

The most common form of interviewing remains the personal interview, a one–on–one meeting with the immediate supervisor or a member of the Human Resources Department. If it is a preliminary interview, it is usually brief giving you and the interviewer an idea of whether or not the position is right for you. During a selection interview, your 'fit' with the company will be analyzed and you must convince the employer you are the best candidate for the job.

 Prior to an interview write out and practice giving answers to questions you are uncomfortable or have difficulty with. If possible have someone review your responses and, more importantly, your "body language." Often our physical reactions say more than our words.

 "Is it a coincidence that the word improvement begins "I"?"

Jean Pare, *Company's Coming Holiday Entertaining*

Tip List

- Practice your responses to potential questions before each interview, especially ones you are uncomfortable with.

- Dress appropriately.

- Be aware of your body language. Be sure to portray confidence in yourself and enthusiasm about the position.

Panel Interviews

If you are successful and progress through the preliminary interview, you will often be faced with a panel interview. It is becoming standard procedure to have several people participate in the interview process; a human resources representative, a member of the department you would be working for, perhaps as your direct supervisor, and as many as three other people who have an interest in who is being hired. Believe it or not, this is to your benefit! The more people who participate in your interview, the greater the chance you have of creating a lasting, positive impression with at least one of them.

There once was a man from Caldeer
Who wanted this job it was clear
He got a little off track
When he bought a six pack
And offered to bribe the employer with beer!

Tip List

- Look at each person when responding to questions. All the panel members are interested in your responses.

- Relax! There are more people present to notice if you are nervous, so pretend they are a group of friends you are chatting with.

- Ask questions throughout the interview. It will give you a break from speaking, and you will also come across as confident and interested in the position.

There are many styles of interviewing and every organization has its own interviewing practices. During your job search you might be exposed to any combination of these formats. Approach each with enthusiasm and energy and you will inevitably be successful!

Chapter 2

Becoming An Active Participant

Observe people you know to be positive and effective communicators: determine what makes them effective and incorporate some of their successful techniques into your own communications.

The job interview is a **two way process.** Both you and the employer are forming opinions, on whether they want you and you want them. It is important that you have enough information about the company to not only impress **them** with your knowledge, but also to allow you to decide if they are the company for you.

"Hasn't she got a lot of drive? She goes forward by patting herself on the back."

Jean Pare, *Company's Coming Barbecues*

Preparing for Your Interview

You received that call asking you to come for an interview so now your work is done, right? . . . WRONG! The most important work remains to be done **during** the interview.

There are strategies you can follow to ensure you are relaxed, prepared and at your peak during the interview. You have worked hard to get as far as the interview stage, so don't quit working now. You must do everything you can to be prepared . . .

Research

Yes, research. Nothing prepares you for unexpected questions or impresses an interviewer more than the fact that you took time to learn about their organization. Information you gather will help you determine what the company is looking for in an employee and enable you to ask informed questions during the interview.

 "It's not easy to achieve freedom without chaos."

Anais Nin

What?

It is important to find out as much about the company as possible when conducting your research. Look for information on:

- What the company specializes in.
- What the company's mission statement is and what their goals are.
- Who they serve.
- The company's reputation with their customers and competition.
- If the company has subsidiaries or a parent company.
- The qualifications of existing staff.
- How many people work for the company.
- The position salary range.

Prepare your list of questions prior to starting your research and continue to add to your list. Write down what you discover. It is easy to forget the company sells shoelaces on the side as you gather more and more information. You will be surprised at the amount of information you find.

Where?

Surprisingly enough, it is fairly easy to gather information on any organization if you are persistent and know where to look.

The Company Itself

Call and speak to the personnel office or even the receptionist in the department where you are being interviewed. Be sure to have your list of questions ready so you don't waste anyone's time.

Company Pamphlets and Publications

Information available to the general public should not be overlooked, for it usually describes a company and their services.

Chamber of Commerce

People in the business can provide the best information on various companies. The information they provide is often very subjective, but it can give you the best indication of what the company is really like.

 Join your local Chamber of Commerce. You will make valuable contacts—maybe even with the company considering hiring you.

Library or Labour Market Information Center

You will be impressed with the information available at your local library in everything from magazines to back–dated newspapers. Ask the librarian to help you locate relevant information.

 Make a list of at least ten positive things that happen to you each day. It is a great idea to supplement your list with positive things you do for other people. You will be surprised and encouraged by how something this simple can change your outlook.

Better Business Bureau

Check into the company's reputation. Are they a company you would feel comfortable working for?

Other Companies

Talk to companies that use the organization's services. What do they think of the company?

Unions

Speak with a union delegate representing the company's employees. What reputation does the organization have with its own staff?

"The more clear you are on what you want, the more power you will have."

Dr. Robert Anthony, _Think On_

Computer Networks

If you have access to a computer, use available network services. Often you can find specific information on larger companies, or you can send out a question into 'computer land' and ask people to respond with information they have. You might be surprised at how many people communicate through computer networks and how helpful they are! The technology is there, use it to your advantage, you may meet someone who can really help!

Remember to be professional when communicating through computers. Someone within the company you are interested in may be responding to your request.

Prepare Questions

After your research is complete, you may find you have discovered a lot about the organization, but still prepare questions to ask during the interview. It may seem odd to be asking questions when you are the one being interviewed, but an interview is a **two–way process.** Asking questions during an interview shows a genuine interest in the company.

What?

Ask questions about:

- The company: Is it expanding? What are their plans and goals for the future? How many people are employed with the company?

- What the position entails: What is a typical day like? What would your duties and responsibilities be? Who would you report to? Who would report to you? How will your skills be used?

- Opportunities for advancement. (Be careful, you do not want to appear to be out to snatch the employer's position.)

- Other questions you have about the company, the position, and your future with them.

- The industry itself: Is this a growing industry?

Avoid asking questions solely about salary, holidays, benefits and company 'perks'. If your only question is "When will I get a raise?," the employer will not be impressed. You will sound like your only concern is with what the organization can do for you, not what you can offer them.

"On your way through life don't worry if you stumble now and then. Only worms can't fall down."

Jean Pare, *Company's Coming Muffins and More*

Rehearsal

Yes, rehearse! Respond to questions out loud, especially those you anticipate having difficulties with **(See Interview Questions).** Not only will this help you give smooth, well thought out answers during the interview, it will also put you in the right frame of mind for 'selling' yourself effectively.

Checklist

Here is a list of things you should prepare **prior to** the morning of your interview. You should add the additional items **you** need for your interview to your list:

- Have enough copies of your resume for each interviewer plus two extra copies: one for yourself and one should an additional person join the interview.
- Have a list of your references and extra copies.
- Take a pen (one you cannot nervously click!) and paper.

Be sure you have the correct phone numbers and addresses of your references. Notify them and discuss the position you have applied for.

- Have your list of questions neatly written out so you can read them.
- Lay out the clean, pressed clothes you plan to wear.
- Have your briefcase packed by the door and ready to go.
- Know the **exact** location of the office you are going to.
- Plan your route to the interview, and check the bus schedule if you are taking public transportation.
- Determine where you will park, as well as an alternate site.
- Other _____

If given a choice, choose the **first** interview; you set the standard for those who follow.

Relax

Now you are prepared. You **know** you will do a great job in the interview, so do something for yourself. Go for a walk, rent a movie, or take a bubble bath. Then **set your alarm** and get some sleep . . . you will be great!

The Interview Day

You may feel nervous or a little pressured the day of your interview. It is essential that you are organized ahead of time so you do not find yourself running frantically around ten minutes before you need to leave. There is no better way to guarantee you will be frazzled during your interview than to start the day off rushed and disorganized.

"Opportunities are usually disguised as hard work, so most people don't recognize them."

Ann Landers

Your checklist should ensure most things are ready the night before the interview. The morning of your interview there are only a few things that are important to remember.

Personal Grooming

Believe it or not, this is where many people get in trouble.

Ladies

When in doubt, be conservative: conservative dress, accessories, make-up and perfume. Remember, if you normally wear perfume you may not be as sensitive to the smell as others. If you must wear scent the day of your interview, spray it in the air in front of you and walk through it. You want your personality to have impact, not your perfume!

There once was a woman from Tribooned.
Who enjoyed smelling heavily perfumed.
She sprayed too much scent,
And to her interview went,
Where from the first "sniff" her
meeting was doomed!

If you do not normally wear make–up, don't feel you must apply it for an interview. Most likely you will end up with less than perfect results or you will be self–conscious about it. A natural look is best, and it's always better to wear too little make–up than too much. Remember, you want the interviewer to be paying attention to what you say, not marvelling at the length of your false lashes!

Try your outfit on ahead of time and practice sitting and standing. Does it hang open, is it hard to sit in, is the collar tight, is it clean? . . . Is it YOU?!

As for clothing, nothing is written in stone about whether women should wear pants or a skirt to an interview. The rule of thumb is: Wear what makes **you** comfortable, what makes you feel like "you."

Gentlemen

You must be comfortable for an interview, so don't feel you must wear a suit if you are not used to wearing one. A sports jacket with a shirt and tie is a good idea, though. You can be more relaxed in a sports jacket and still look professional.

As with women, be sure to use cologne sparingly. The last thing you want is for the interviewer to remember you only because their hand still smells like your cologne at the end of the day!

 Visit the work site prior to your interview to see what employees are wearing. Choose an outfit slightly more formal than what is worn in the office.

Body Language

You have taken the time to dress professionally. Be sure your body language also projects a professional image.

Eye Contact

Good eye contact conveys confidence and enthusiasm, and makes you appear more credible.

Facial Expression

Smile! Imagine yourself as an interviewer meeting people all day. Everyone begins to look the same—until you walk in with a refreshingly friendly, energetic and smiling face. You will be remembered!

Energy Level

Show enthusiasm for the position and try to be energetic. (Remember the tired employer who has been interviewing all day.)

Posture

Maintain good posture through the entire interview keeping your shoulders square yet relaxed.

 Take ten minutes in front of the mirror, or even a video camera, and give convincing examples of your skills. Be sure your body language agrees with what your mouth is saying, i.e. watch for nervous gestures and expressions (umm, etc.), or lack of eye contact.

Smoking

On an interview morning, perhaps more than any other morning, you may want to have a cigarette. **Avoid the temptation.** If you absolutely must smoke, do it before you get dressed. Avoid smoking immediately before you go in to an interview and in the car on the way there. Cigarette smoke lingers on your clothes, breath, and hands long after the cigarette is gone, and breath mints and cologne do a poor job covering it up.

"Success is getting up one more time."

Dr. Robert Anthony, *Think On*

The smell of nicotine can be very offensive to the non–smoking interviewer and you do not want to start off your interview on the wrong foot. You need everyone in the room on your side.

Alcohol

"The present is the only thing that has no end."

Erwin Schrodinger

Everyone has their own way to relax for an interview. If relaxing for you means a quick shot of scotch before leaving the house, stop and think. Although the effects of alcohol may be calming, they may also be impairing and you need all your wits about you for an interview. And, as with cigarette smoke, the odor of alcohol lingers long after you drink it. A job candidate who smells like alcohol will **not** be hired.

Travel Time

Be sure you know exactly where the building is you are going to and how long it will take you to drive there. Have money ready for parking. Leave early enough to allow for the worst traffic conditions and never park at a parking meter. You do not want to be thinking about the parking ticket you are getting while you should be relating your great skills to an interviewer.

There once was a man from Cantuckee
Who came for an interview at three
But what a mistake
He showed up a week late
We sure didn't hire him, did we??

Arrival Time

Plan to arrive at least 15 minutes early so you have time to relax, catch your breath and compose your thoughts. It is better to be early and wait than be late and miss the opportunity to get your dream job.

Some of these suggestions may seem trivial when you read them, but they are things you may not think about when you are nervous and concentrating on landing a job.

"Opportunities always look bigger going away than coming."

Jean Pare, *Company's Coming Salads*

Take the time to plan ahead. Even if you are not normally a list–maker, draw up a list and schedule your time the day of an interview. Your day will run more smoothly and you will be glad you were prepared . . . Trust us!

Chapter 3

The Interview

You have worked hard to make it to this stage of the job search and you deserve to congratulate yourself. Any time you feel frustrated, discouraged or nervous, think of the number of people who applied for this position. **You** are among the few chosen for an interview.

"Think of it—You can walk a mile and yet only move two feet."

Jean Pare, *Company's Coming Muffins and More*

You are now ready to begin the interview. All the planning and preparation you have done so far will make your meeting run much smoother, but this is still the critical point. You only have one chance to sell yourself and now is the time to do it!

Stages of the Interview

The formal job interview is designed to be as in-depth and comprehensive as possible, with a maximum of information being exchanged. Indeed, this is in your best interest and that of the company. Neither you nor your potential employer wants to spend the time and effort that go into hiring and training, only to find within a few months you are unsuited for the position.

"It takes 20 years to make an overnight success."

Eddie Cantor

Each interview you attend will be unique, but most interviews follow a standard progression.

Greeting the Receptionist

Although not all companies have receptionists, there will usually be someone who greets you when you arrive for the interview (10–15 minutes early of course!). It is essential you treat this person with respect and courtesy. Even though they may not be directly involved with your interview, their casual remarks to the person responsible for hiring could be critical. Eight out of ten employers will ask the receptionist's opinion of interview candidates. Be sure the opinion of you is favorable.

Engage the receptionist in some small talk. Be polite and friendly but be careful to not interrupt their work or overdo it and appear 'sleazy.'

Introductions

Inevitably, the time will come for you to meet the interviewer(s). Don't forget to smile and walk tall and confidently. The moment you enter the room, before you have even said a word, your interview has begun and you are being evaluated.

Remember:

It only takes five seconds to make an impression of you, make sure it is a good one.

As a courtesy, wait until the employer invites you to sit down before you take your seat.

Handshake

Whether you are a man or woman, be sure to offer your hand when you greet the interviewers. It is both professional and courteous to do so.

Practice shaking hands with a friend. Be sure your shake is firm but not too strong. The only thing worse than a limp handshake is a painful one. Establish eye contact while you shake hands. This makes your meeting more memorable and helps you remember names!

Names

Try to remember each interviewer's name so you can be more personal when talking during the meeting. Making the effort to remember and use names can have a positive and impressive impact.

Repeat each interviewers' name as you shake hands. This will help you remember them; ie: "Hello Chris, nice to meet you."

Small Talk

It is a good idea to engage in small talk before the formal part of the interview begins. By beginning your interview on a casual note, you put yourself and the employer at ease. You may comment on the weather or the look of the office, but refrain from discussing problems you had on the way to the interview, such as how you had to speed to make it on time.

Be sensitive to employers' time restrictions and interest in what you are discussing. Do not continue speaking just for the sake of talking.

 Pick at least three of your work–related skills and write down two concrete, positive examples of how you have used those skills in the past. If you cannot think of examples from the workplace, draw from your volunteer or extra curricular activities.

Information Exchange

After you have arrived and exchanged pleasantries, the more formal part of the interview begins. You will be expected to respond to questions in an **honest** and **thorough** manner. It is very important you provide **informative** and **complete** answers without boring the employer. Skilled interviewers will pose open-ended questions, but it is up to you to offer enough information to provide them with a sense of who you are.

 Don't be afraid to laugh and relax in an interview . . . Be yourself!!

Remember:

One word 'Yes' or 'No' responses are **forbidden.** They provide no information to the employer. The only thing they accomplish is a very short interview.

Try relaxing, smiling and being friendly throughout the interview. Leave the employer with the memory of your smiling face, not a scowling or uncomfortable one.

**One woman thought her luck was so tough
She took pride in never saying much stuff
In the interview her crime
Was saying just 'yes' all the time
She wasn't hired 'cause she didn't say enough!**

The information exchange is the most important part of your interview. Sample questions to help you prepare are provided in **Interview Questions and Responses.**

It is important you ask the questions you have prepared.

Final Summary

Eventually employers will come to the point where they have no further questions and feel they have a good idea of who you are and what you have to offer. But before the interview ends **you** must ensure that you feel comfortable leaving.

Maintain good eye contact throughout the interview, scanning all interviewers. Good eye contact conveys genuine interest and confidence.

- Have you left a copy of your references?
- Have you asked all the questions you have prepared?

Space your questions throughout the interview so you do not have a long list at the end. If your questions have not been answered, however, do not leave until they are.

Again, you must make sure you have enough information about the company, the position, the duties and the responsibilities to make a decision about whether you want to work for them.

• Have you provided enough information about yourself?

If you forgot to mention something, or feel the employer does not have a good sense of the skills you have to offer, bring them to the employer's attention. You only get one chance to sell yourself. Make sure you do it now and with enough impact to be remembered.

Some questions need to be asked tactfully and not too early in the interview.

 If at the end of an interview you feel you have not given enough information to be seriously considered for the position be prepared to add information in a closing remark.

These include questions about salary, benefits, and vacation time, as well as any other questions you have about controversial company policies.

Remember, your goal is to provide a good impression of yourself. Do not ruin it by appearing only interested in the salary and perks, or by bringing up controversial company issues.

• Offer a closing remark highlighting your strongest skills and qualities.

Leaving the employer on a positive note is as important as making a good first impression. Offer a brief summary of your strengths and attributes which make **you** the perfect choice for the position. State how interested you are in working for the company and show your enthusiasm and drive.

Closing the Interview

When both you and the employer are finished asking questions and you have nothing further to offer, it is time to close the interview.

"It is much easier to keep up than to catch up."

Dr. Robert Anthony, *Think On*

Before leaving remember to:

- Ask when you may call to find out if a decision has been made. Do not leave it to the employer to do this. Show your interest and initiative by being the one who calls.

- Thank the employer for their time, smile, and offer your hand again.

- **Leave.** This does not mean be in a hurry and flee, especially if you do not feel you have said everything you want. It means know when it is time to leave and do not overstay your welcome.

Remember:

Be considerate of the employer's time restraints and job demands.

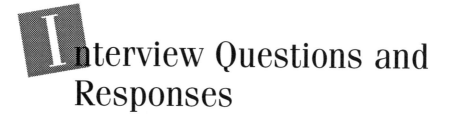Interview Questions and Responses

The following are examples of questions you **may** be asked in an interview. Remember, these are very general and every interview is different. Of course, there will also be questions designed to test your knowledge of your specific field.

"Discipline doesn't have to be about restriction, it can be about freedom, it can be about openness, it can be about more rather than less."

Batya Zamir

Develop your own answers prior to the interview. Although we give sample responses, your situation is unique and no one answer will be correct in every situation. Give strong responses that leave a great impression!

How?

Elaborate answers and give *concrete examples* so employers have a good understanding of what you have to offer.

**There was a job candidate from Kildare
Who when nervous would just twist her hair,
She became so distraught,
In her hair her fingers got caught
We cut them out with ever so much care!**

Listen to yourself and let your voice and expressions project the enthusiasm you feel for the position. Maintain good *eye contact* throughout the interview, scanning *all* the interviewers: they all are interested in your responses. Good eye contact conveys genuine interest and enthusiasm.

The most important thing to remember about an interview is that you only have one chance, so sell yourself as much as you possibly can. There is nothing worse than leaving an interview thinking, "I wish I would have mentioned . . ."

Remember:

Not all interviewers are skilled and experienced. Often they may be as nervous as you during the interview, and things may not always go as smoothly as you would expect. Try to be calm and pleasant and **always** be professional, no matter how it is going. You may not land the job this time, but if you have a great interview they will remember you when a position that is just right for you comes up.

Tell me about yourself.

This is often one of the first questions in an interview. It is an open-ended question designed to give you the opportunity to talk about yourself and relax. Unfortunately, it usually has the opposite effect. It is up to you whether you discuss your work or personal life, or a combination of both. Choosing a combination will give the interviewer a well–rounded picture of **you.** It gives you an opportunity to highlight your relevant skills and experience, and if you are lucky you can mention how much you enjoy "underwater basket weaving" and—surprise!—one of the interviewers has recently taken a course. Now you have an ally, someone who will remember you, and you can relax.

 Give enough information for an employer to get an impression of you but do not give your entire life and employment history. 2–3 minutes should be enough.

What type of salary do you expect for this position?

"I am sure your company has a range and I am willing to negotiate within that range." If you are pushed for a 'bottom line' be sure to indicate a range, i.e. $1200–$1500 per month. You have completed research on the company, so you have a good idea what the range is. Nothing will eliminate you faster from a competition than a poor answer to the salary question, whether it be too high or too low.

What are your goals for the next year or 2 years or 5 years?

Describe your career goals, and what you can do for the company and for yourself. You want the interviewer to know you will work hard for their company, but you do not want them to feel that you are out to get their job.

 Create a mock interview with a friend, responding to questions as you would in a real situation. Videotaping this is a great idea. There is no better way to improve your interview skills than to see on film how you present to others.

Why should we hire you?

This is your opportunity to convince the employer you are the best person for the job. Detail how you have the skills, personality, and enthusiasm to excel in the position. This is not the time to be shy. The next person being interviewed won't be!

 **There once was a girl from Cantinking,
Who during her interview seemed to be shrinking
Imagine the surprise
When she slid from our eyes
to the floor, where perhaps she lay thinking.**

Tell me about your last employer.

Above all else, *be positive*. If there was a problem, *do not* go into it! If you discuss the problems you had on your previous job or bad mouth past employers, what will you say about this employer if you leave them? Respond by saying "They were great to work with," and end the discussion.

What do you consider to be your strengths?

Pick three of your strengths you can relate to the position and emphasize them with examples. Take enough time to answer this question *thoroughly*. *Do not* sell yourself short. Take credit for the things you have worked hard to achieve!

What are your weaknesses?

This is a tricky question, but you can take a weakness and turn it into a strength. "I get very involved with customers, but they receive excellent service as a result." Do not describe a weakness without turning it into a positive attribute or without saying how you are working to overcome it. Discuss no more than two. You want to emphasize your strengths, not your weaknesses.

Why did you leave your last job?
Why are you leaving your current position?

Be Positive.

Perhaps you are looking for a position with more challenge or room to grow. If you were laid off, that's fine. Company restructuring is very common these days.

"In general, there are two kinds of people who make mistakes: those who won't admit them, and those who call them experience."

Bits & Pieces Aug. '92

If you were fired from your position be honest. You never want to be hired on the basis of a lie, because the truth will eventually come out. The key to answering is to **be prepared** and do not say too much. Never say anything bad about your past employer and never go into too much detail. There are a number of ways to respond:

- If you were fired after less than six months, simply say that you made a mistake taking the position and it turned out to be a poor match.

- If it was after more than six months, there may have been a change in your duties that didn't work out or a management change resulted in a conflict of values.

Admit that you were fired, acknowledge that some type of mistake was made, and state you have learned from the experience.

What do you consider your major life accomplishments?

This question sums up what you consider to be important in your life. If you mention the first time you used your brother's ID to get into a bar or the day your divorce became final, an employer would be wise to question the type of ethics you would embrace as an employee. Choosing career–related accomplishments is a good idea.

What are your hobbies? What do you do in your spare time?

An employer wants to know if you are a well–rounded individual with outside interests.

Identify three weaknesses you have and turn them into positive strengths. Always maintain a positive attitude when doing this: i.e. "I am a perfectionist. I feel this is a strength, however, as it encourages my co–workers to strive for perfection."

Alternate: What was the last book you read or movie you saw?

Again, if it was an Archie comic or a slasher movie, the employer may wonder about the scope of your interests!

How do you handle stress?

Give examples of what you do when you go home after a stress–filled day. "I go for a walk or a run, cook, do crafts . . ." etc. Employers want to know if you have ways of relaxing after work so you can return refreshed the next day. If you have worked in an especially stress–filled atmosphere, give examples of how you coped with the stress at work.

Alternate: Tell me about a situation where you were under stress. How did you handle it?

"What we do in our leisure time is almost as important as what we do during working hours."

Bits & Pieces **March '90**

Are you a good problem solver?

Illustrate, with examples, how you are able to communicate and discuss things effectively with co–workers, superiors, and subordinates. Emphasize that you take initiative to resolve problems on your own.

"Every exit is an entry somewhere."

Tom Stoppard

How is your job search going? How long have you been unemployed?

Be honest, but be positive. An employer does not want to hear you are desperate to work and ready to accept anything! Outline the steps you are taking to gain employment, and emphasize that you are taking time to make sure the company you accept employment with is one to whom you can be committed. Discuss how you are expanding your network, meeting people, upgrading your skills, and researching alternatives.

Alternate: What is your approach to your job search?

What type of supervision do you work most effectively under?

Employers want to know if you can work independently as well as take direction. This is a good time to talk about how self–motivated you are, what type of team player you are, and how you communicate with authority figures. Again, highlight your strengths, illustrate how well you work in a variety of situations, and do not sell yourself short!

"Minds are like parachutes: they only function when open."

Bits & Pieces, Aug. '92

Alternate: What do you expect from a supervisor?

Again, illustrate how well you work in various situations.

Describe a situation where you disagreed with someone at work. How did you handle it?

The interviewer is looking to see that the problem was managed in a mature fashion and a compromise was reached. It is important that you can effectively resolve problems without running to your supervisor.

"What you do speaks so loud that I cannot hear what you say."

Ralph Waldo Emerson

What do you know about our company?

Let's hope you have done your research, for now is your chance to show what you have learned!

"Moving fast is not the same as going somewhere."

Dr. Robert Anthony, Think On

Describe your major disappointments or failures?

Like the weakness question, you will want to identify one failure and turn it into something positive. "The promotion I had worked very hard for was given to someone else. However, I subsequently discussed this with my employer, discovered why it was given to the other person, and went on to produce work that was more consistent with what was wanted."

Do you have a personal motto or philosophy you live by?

Employers aren't necessarily looking for something profound. Rather they want to uncover something that reflects your attitude toward work, people or goal setting. If your personal motto is "Work to Surf," you should probably refrain from sharing it!

"No mistake is fatal unless you make it so."

Dr. Robert Anthony, *Think On*

Think of someone you dislike. What do you dislike about them?

Keep your answer general and *do not* focus on any one particular individual. The employer wants to learn how you get along with others. If you come up with a list of people you dislike, they may correctly assume you are not an effective team player. Discuss qualities or characteristics which you do not like and are not desirable in a work setting. Then show that you do not possess these characteristics. "I dislike people who are always late, because punctuality is important to me."

What was the last course or seminar you attended?

An employer is looking to see whether or not you are continuing your education and attempting to remain current in a changing marketplace. Describe recent courses you have taken or explain to the employer you understand the necessity of learning and expanding your education. Explain that you do this through other means, such as reading, discussion groups, educational videos, etc.

While pursuing our HR man with zest,
A young interviewee was becoming a pest;
In a restaurant he did sob
How he needed the job,
He wasn't hired as you could have guessed.

How would you feel about working for someone younger than you?

"Age is not a factor. Everyone has something positive to add to a position and there would certainly be no problem."

Outline your computer experience for me, please.

This is a straightforward question—if you have computer experience. Be certain to give the *accurate* names and editions of the programs you are familiar with, for example, Microsoft Word 5.1. If you do not have any computer experience, and it is necessary for the position, be sure to indicate the steps you are taking to learn the required material. If at all possible, take some computer training now. It will enhance your resume, be good for your self–esteem and expand your network!

Make sure the message on your answering machine sounds professional.

A co–worker is continually taking credit for work *you* have done. What do you do?

This situation can be very uncomfortable. Again, the employer wants to see if you would handle the situation without disrupting the office. There are a number of ways you could manage the situation. First, discuss this in private with the individual in a professional and diplomatic manner. Second, you could subtly check back with your supervisor to discuss your progress or request feedback. This way you receive feedback and ensure the supervisor is aware the work is yours.

Is your career where you expected it would be at this point in your life? Why or why not?

This seems to be a personal question but really it is not. An employer is simply looking to see whether you set personal goals and work hard to achieve them. Indeed, you may not achieve every goal you set for yourself, but that should not stop you from setting them, working hard to achieve them and re–adjusting them if and when necessary.

**There once was a woman from Dundeen,
Who was creative on her message machine.
Our HR Manager called,
with her message was appalled,
For that position she never was seen!**

Do you feel your education has helped or hindered your career? How?

Any education you have received over the years has helped your work history, either directly or indirectly. Education helps expand perspective, increase awareness, and enlighten us to new possibilities. Learning is a life–long process and any employer would be pleased to hear of any extra–curricular learning you are doing.

If chosen for this position, how will you go about familiarizing yourself with our policies, procedures, and other employees?

The answer *you* give will be unique. Everyone gathers information and meets people in a different manner. An employer wants to hear you will take initiative and have a game plan other than sitting at your desk waiting for the office Welcome Wagon! Show you do not need someone to take time away from their own duties just to hold your hand for the first three weeks.

Interviewers agree: past behaviour is the best indicator of future performance. In other words, interviewers ask how you reacted in past situations to see how you will perform in the future.

Do you consider yourself a quick learner? Give an example.

Remember, always be positive. Think of an example, even if it is not work–related. Maybe you just learned to play squash and won your first game. When we work we learn new things daily and an employer wants to be sure you can keep on top of things.

It's 4 o'clock on Friday and your computer crashes, taking with it a presentation you scheduled for Monday morning. What will you do?

There are two solutions to this problem. You could go home and forget about it until Monday, call everyone at the last minute and re–schedule. Or you could get your computer running, finish the presentation and go ahead as planned, without disrupting anyone else's schedule. (Mention that you will also save your work faithfully so if the computer does crash again you will lose very little!) As an employer, which solution would you rather hear?

You discover a co–worker stealing company property. What do you do?

This is a challenging question. Does your answer depend on what they are stealing? Are pencils okay but computer programs off–limits? Stealing company property accounts for an astonishing amount of lost revenue for a company. Often we find ourselves caught in the mind set of, "well everyone does it . . . " As a result, we tend to dismiss it. That probably is not a good answer.

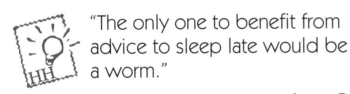

"The only one to benefit from advice to sleep late would be a worm."

Jean Pare, *Company's Coming Muffins and More*

Your answer should outline that you understand the consequences of employee theft, how it hurts all those involved with the organization and you would make an effort to explain this to the employee involved. Running to management and informing them of every missing paper clip is not the solution, however.

If you are currently unemployed and looking for employment, develop a positive response to the all–too–common question of, "what do you do for a living?" This will help you develop your network and save you from any awkward situations.

You and your boss often don't see eye to eye. You are passed over for a promotion you thought you deserved. What do you do?

The underlying issue of this question is not specifically what you would do if passed over for a promotion, but what you do when something in the workplace is bothering you. Do you blame someone else, saying "My boss and I don't get along that's why I never got the promotion." Or do you handle such situations constructively by dealing with them? An employer wants to know you will deal with issues and concerns you have in a positive manner and then get on with things. Structure your answer accordingly.

 Offer interviewers extra copies of your resume. This illustrates how well-prepared you are and also shows initiative at the outset of the interview.

Do you consider yourself management material? Why or why not?

When you are thinking about your answer to this question remember that business would not run if everyone was a colonel and there were no soldiers to carry out the orders. Regardless of whether or not we aspire to be management, we all have significant skills to offer.

How often do you feel you deserve a salary increase? Why?

This question can be quite misleading. Remember, your potential employer knows relatively little about your work habits and you are already telling them you need or deserve regular salary increases. Perhaps the best answer to this question is to say you believe salary increases should not be taken for granted, but earned with job performance. If the job you are applying for is a union position you will have predetermined pay increases and will not be asked this question.

 "Most of us would like an occupation that wouldn't keep us occupied."

Jean Pare, *Company's Coming Barbecues*

A fellow staff member continually puts you down and embarrasses you in front of other staff. What do you do?

The best solution would be to take control of the situation without disrupting the running of the office. Employers know this kind of thing can be harmful to office morale and needs to be handled quickly and professionally. Talk to the individual privately and tell them how you are feeling. Perhaps their motives are not as under–handed as you had thought. Either way, you have not sunk to their level, you have handled yourself professionally and paved the way for a more positive working environment.

 Avoid saying you would immediately go to the boss. A potential employer wants to know you can handle issues and problems on your own.

Describe a project you were involved in from start to finish. What was your role?

You must be prepared for this question in advance. Take the time to review your experiences and accomplishments prior to an interview so you can be assured you will have many examples to draw on. When describing your role, be sure to give yourself credit where due and do not be afraid to pat yourself on the back.

 "If at first you don't succeed, you're about average."

Dr. Robert Anthony, *Think On*

What do you consider the three most important qualities a company you work for should have?

The answer to this question will be different for everyone, but it should encompass some of the qualities the company has (thank goodness you have completed your company research). These qualities could be anything: growth, stability, diversity, room for promotion, positive vision for the future, employee profit sharing, total quality management philosophy, friendly employees, etc..

Your supervisor has just explained something to you for the second time and you still don't understand. What do you do?

Do you simply bumble through and hope you get it sort of right? Do you ask your supervisor to explain it yet again? Or do you acknowledge the fact that people communicate in different fashions and simply ask someone else? A potential employer wants to see that you acknowledge and understand your limitations and the limitations of others, but are innovative enough to get beyond them and still get the task done. Whatever you do, do not simply say "Well, I would think I was stupid if I couldn't understand. I would ask my supervisor to give the project to someone else." That is absolutely the worst answer.

**There was once a young man from Guller;
Who had a very poor sense of color;
For his interview he was seen,
Wearing blue orange and green,
He should have sought the opinion of another!**

Are you a leader or a follower? Give an example. What role do you consider more important in a company environment?

Not everyone in a company can be a leader and not everyone can be a follower. It is essential that you recognize your own strengths and realize the importance of there being both leaders and followers in a company. Again, think of concrete examples to illustrate your strengths prior to the interview so you are not caught off guard by this question.

Remember:

This is only a *sample* of questions you might be asked, but they provide insight into what interviewers are looking for. The answers given are only guidelines, and the ones you provide must reflect YOUR situation, qualifications, and personality.

Off-Limit Questions

There are questions that are by their nature too personal and interviewers must refrain from asking.

What?

It is not proper for an interviewer to ask you questions regarding your:

Age

Health

Religious Affiliation

Marital Status

Family Status

Ethnicity

Financial Standing

Sexual Orientation

 A thank–you note after your meeting is an effective and courteous way to ensure that an employer remembers you.

Although these questions are prohibited in order to protect you from any interviewer bias or prejudice, an interviewer who really wants to know will find a way to ask. It is your decision whether or not to answer or accept a position within the company.

Whatever your choice, retain your **good humor** and be **open-minded,** an interviewer may simply be making conversation with no intent to offend or put you on the defensive.

 These guidelines may differ between states, provinces and countries. Use them only as a general reference and research interviewer's limitations in your area prior to an interview.

You made it! Your interview is now complete. You have done a great job. Now go home, take the rest of the day off, and reward yourself by doing something for you!

Follow Up

"Habit is habit, and not to be flung
out of the window by any man,
but coaxed downstairs a step at
a time."

Mark Twain

You made a great impression during the interview, so make sure it lasts!
It is important to stay in contact, not only to see how the competition
is going, but also to remind the employer of who you are. If the choice
is between you and another candidate, you may be chosen because you
kept in contact with the company and they heard your name more
than the other person's. Again, please be sensitive to how busy an
employer is. **Do not harass them!**

Thank You Card

Immediately following an interview send a thank you card. Address it
to ALL interviewers or send one to each interviewer (another reason to
remember names.)

If you send a thank–you card by mail,
send it the day of, or the day after, the
interview: it will take a couple of days to
get there. If possible, hand–deliver your
card one to three days after the interview.

Write a short note outlining:

- Your thanks for the employer taking the time to see you.
- Relevant information you forgot to mention in the interview.
- The skills which make **you** the perfect choice.
- Your genuine interest in the position.

 Keep it brief and interesting. You *will* be remembered.

A prompt thank–you:

Leaves the employer with a positive impression of you as someone considerate and appreciative of the time they have spent with you.

Gives you a chance to re–emphasize the interest you have in the position and re–state specific skills qualifying you for the position—especially ones the employer suggested would be useful.

Provides the opportunity to mention anything you forgot during the interview.

Keeps your name fresh in the mind of the interviewer.

Thank–you cards are becoming more popular and you may not be the only candidate sending one. Wouldn't you prefer to be one of the people who sends a thank–you, rather than one of the few who do not?

Call Back

You took the time to find out when to call back. Now make sure to do so on the date indicated. If you don't, it will appear as if you have lost interest in the position. If you forgot to ask when a decision was being made, call back **within the week** to see how the competition is progressing. This way you will appear interested and enthusiastic.

"To err is human, To forgive takes restraint; To forget you forgave Is the mark of a Saint."

Suzanne Douglass

Make your call directly to one of the interviewers and keep it brief. Ask if a decision has been made and if not, mention the details you highlighted in your thank–you card. Set another time when you may call again.

Do not become a pest by calling too frequently or talking for too long, but do not let the employer forget who you are.

eedback

Request feedback on your interview whether you are chosen for the position or not. Employers may be uncomfortable providing this information, so it is up to you to phrase your questions so the employer can comfortably answer.

How?

When speaking with the employer ask:

- Why the employer made the choice they did.

- What skills, qualifications, education and experience does the person who was hired have.

- What you could have improved on or done differently in the interview during the interview. It is better to find out now what you did wrong than to continue making the same mistakes in all interviews.

- What you did well during the interview. It is also important to find out what you did well so you continue doing these things.

"The learned person is not the one who gives the right answer, but the one who asks the right questions."

Claude Lévi–Strauss

 If the employer does not want to provide feedback, thank them for their time anyway. Leaving your meeting on a positive note will leave the door open for future contact.

Remember:

Hard work, determination, persistence, and skill will land you your next job.

Chapter 5

You're Offered the Job...Now What?

So you have been offered a job. Congratulations! Now what? Well, do you want the position? This sounds like an unusual question, but remember: you interviewed the company at the same time they were interviewing you.

"There are two ways we can meet a difficulty: either we can alter the difficulty or we can alter ourselves to meet it."

Bits & Pieces, Jan. '90

Ask Yourself . . .

• Does it seem like an organization you could work for?

• Is the company's vision of the future consistent with yours?

• Are you comfortable with the position and what it would require of you?

• Have you negotiated a salary agreeable to both of you?

You must have these answered before you jump into a new career. If you feel there are still questions that need to be answered before you accept the position, do not be afraid to ask. It will be better for you and the employer in the long run if you ask them now!

Salary Negotiations

Before accepting any position, you must be sure the salary is one you can live with. Is the company going to compensate you sufficiently for the work you do?

Negotiating your salary can seem intimidating, but like other aspects of the job interview, planning is essential. Never underestimate the influence you may have in determining your salary. You might convince an employer that your qualifications and experience warrant a higher salary than they were initially prepared to offer. It never hurts to try!

"You will never let yourself have more money than you think you are worth."

Dr. Robert Anthony, *Think On*

Your negotiating power varies, as different organizations and jobs have different salary ranges. It is up to you to be prepared.

How?

- Find out how much other companies are paying people with similar qualifications and experience in similar positions. You will not be happy with $20,000 if the employee next door is receiving $30,000.

- Call the personnel department of the company where you are being offered the job and ask for the position salary range.

- Determine prior to your meeting the minimum salary you are willing to accept. If you have your bottom line established, you will not be left calculating during your meeting.

- Review your education and related experience in order to convince the employer you deserve a favorable salary. They chose you as the best candidate, so they must think you are worth a good salary!

It is up to you to be sure your salary is acceptable. Do not stop working yet!

When?

Wait until after you have been offered the position before negotiating your salary. Discussing salary at the beginning of the first interview is premature, but waiting until after you accept the position reduces your negotiating power.

What to Do?

Think of salary negotiations as though you were buying a car. You spent lots of time and effort choosing the right vehicle. You may pay a little extra to get what you want, but you will not pay more than you think the car is worth.

"If you are willing to admit you are wrong when you are wrong, you are all right."

Mildred McAfee

Likewise, you will try to make the best salary deal possible, but you may accept slightly less in order to secure a good position. You chose the job. What will **you** be happy with?

Should you accept less than what you expected, there is the option of asking for a salary review after a set time period, perhaps after a three to six month probationary period. You will not only have your education and experience to fall back on, but also the work you have completed with the company as support for your salary request.

Formalizing Your Job Offer

Your employer will probably give you a formal written job offer. Be sure it outlines the salary and terms you agreed to.

If you are not given a formal offer or if information is missing, write your own acceptance letter outlining the terms you agreed upon.

How?

- Reflect your pleasure and enthusiasm in being offered the position in your opening sentence. Start off on the right foot!

- Casually outline the terms of accepting the position. Be sure to outline everything from salary to salary review dates to holidays and special conditions you agreed to.

- Close the letter by again showing your interest in the position.

**There once was a woman from Van Gump
Who thought she was negotiating her
salary per month
"Twenty-four," the offer went,
But per year they had meant
The sum on her first check left
her stumped.**

Date and sign two copies, give one to your employer and keep the other for yourself to refer to should any discrepancies arise.

This is a good way to make sure you and the employer are clear on the terms of your accepting the position. It is also a nice way to say thank you to the employer.

Contract Positions

"Four little words that aren't heard often enough are, **you may be right.**"

Helen Keller

In today's tight job market, many positions are contract or temporary positions. Should you be offered a contract position, be sure to see the actual contract and read it thoroughly before you start work. If there are clauses you do not understand, have them explained to you or have a lawyer look at the agreement. Be certain of what you are signing, for both your protection and that of the employer. You do not want to enter into an agreement you are not prepared to fulfil.

Getting Started

Should you decide to accept the position, do everything you can to orient yourself quickly so you take as little time as possible to become a productive member of the team.

Do You Know?

- Where everything is located in the office? Ask for a quick tour. Knowing where the washroom and lunch room are will make your first few days much easier!

- What is appropriate office attire? Start off on the right foot by being properly dressed and ready for work.

- What the hours of work are?

- Company policies and procedures regarding: smoking, breaks, office supplies, time off for medical appointments, etc.

- When and how you will be paid?

- When to take holidays and who to inform?

 Many organizations have a manual outlining company policies and procedures. However, if they do not, it is your responsibility to ask.

Although you might not start your primary tasks or major projects right away, keep busy. Do what you can to familiarize yourself with the workings of the office. Take the initiative to find things to do, whether they are your duties or not. People will appreciate your eagerness and helpfulness and you will settle into the office routine more quickly.

 "A happy person is not a person in a certain set of circumstances, but rather a person with a certain set of attitudes."

Hugh Downs

You did it! Now get started and enjoy the job you worked hard to get!

That Was Then...

There are many people who find themselves looking for work for the first time in ten or twenty years. Here is a look at what has changed. In the past:

- Interviews were often only a brief formality before hiring.

- There was rarely a panel or more than one person interviewing.

- The interviewer was normally the individual who would be your direct supervisor.

- Often the decision to hire you had already been made and the interview was a formality, held more to see if you would "fit" in the organization, rather than to see if your qualifications were exact.

- It was unusual to go through more than one interview.

- Interviews were primarily one sided. The interviewer asked questions and did not expect to be questioned by you.

- If you were hired, you often started work that afternoon or the very next day.

- There was rarely more than two or three people interviewed for a position.

- Employers searched desperately for suitable employees.

This Is Now...

- Interview competitions are left open for several weeks to receive applications.

- After a candidate has been hired, they are often not expected to start for two weeks.

- It is standard procedure to go through several interviews before being hired.

- Candidates are often exposed to telephone interviews, computer screenings or videotaped question and answer sessions before being selected to be interviewed in person.

- It is common to be interviewed by at least a three–person panel.

- Interviews are two sided: you are interviewing the company as much as they are interviewing you.

- It may take several days or weeks to hear the results of a competition.

- Employers have many suitable candidates to choose from when filling a position.

Conclusion

You have now completed all the phases of the job interview. If you were not successful at your first interview, review the sections you need to improve on and remember not to become discouraged. You *will* be successful as long as you are willing to practice, learn, and grow!

"Every step is an end, and every step is a fresh beginning."

Johann Wolfgang von Goethe

Once you have been successful and received a job offer, remember it was not luck that got you here, it was hard work, devotion and skill. You have *mastered* the job interview!

Congratulations!

A Look at Another Job Interview: Interview Scenario 2

"Five minutes, just another five minutes," Mike groans, as he rolls over and looks at the clock. It's not that he hates his job, in fact, he loves it. It's just that he hates Monday mornings. Funny how he has to spend the entire week trying to get more sleep because he never gets to bed at a decent hour on Sunday. He has to get going, even though it is dark out and insufferably cold in the bedroom. "I hate winter," he mumbles, as he heads for a quick shower and shave.

 "Happiness is loving what you do and getting someone else to pay you to do it!"

Dr. Robert Anthony, *Think On*

Mike Connors is an idea man, one who had dreamed of being in advertising since the tenth grade. So it was no surprise to anyone when he landed a good job with an ad agency right out of college. College sometimes seemed like a waste of time to Mike, and he had often wanted to skip the theoretical garble and get right into a job. He had stuck it out though and was glad he had. A few of Mike's friends, his best friend included, had skipped college and sometimes regretted it. More and more it seemed like you needed to have that piece of paper *and* know someone in the industry to get a half–decent job. Fortunately, Mike had some connections, thanks to an old drama teacher, and even though he is the low man on the totem pole at work, they treat him like he has potential.

At 8:25 Mike screams in the door, on time, but just barely. He makes a quick mental note to only rent one movie next Sunday.

"Hey Mike, the Anderson/Carter project looked great, I saw some of the drawings Friday." Pat Gartner is a good friend, someone Mike can count on to give support or valid criticism whenever he needs it. "Thanks, Pat, I'll take that as a compliment coming from you," Mike laughs over his shoulder as he heads for his office. The Anderson/Carter deal is a big one and Mike knows he has been lucky to be chosen to head up the project. He has worked hard for them and it looks like everything is going ahead, on schedule and on budget.

Mike is just finishing up the last ad sketch when the phone rings.

"Hello Michael, Ms. Atkins would like to see you." Atkins is technically the boss, but everyone, including Atkins, knows that it is Chris who keeps the ship on course.

 "Doing your best is more important than being your best."

Leadership...with a Human Touch, Volume B #1

"Sure, Chris. I could use the diversion. I'll head right over." Mike likes Atkins and appreciates that she recognizes his potential. She has gone out on a corporate limb, handing a big project to the office rookie, and he has worked hard not to disappoint her.

"Mike, come in and sit down for a minute." Atkins has a comfortable office and a comfortable management style that encourages team work and mutual respect. Mike admires that and it puts him at ease. "I'm impressed with the work you've done on the Anderson/Carter project, Mike. More importantly, *they* are very impressed and that makes this even harder for me. Mike, I have to lay you off today. I know this is sudden, and it in no way reflects your performance here. We've lost a big project that was to start next month, and even the Anderson/ Carter deal has been down–sized. What it comes down to is that I don't have the work or the money coming in to keep you here.

I'm really sorry about this Mike. You know how I feel about your potential in the industry and I hate to give you up. I'll be more than happy to write you a glowing reference letter."

 Many industries are unstable these days. Do not assume your job is forever. Keep your resume and training current just in case.

Atkins is genuinely disturbed by all of this. Mike can see that, but it doesn't make it any less of a shock for him.

Be sure to ask for reference letters whenever you leave an organization. The people you worked for will not be there forever.

"Today is officially your last day. I'll have a check ready for you by 4:30. We'll pay you through the end of the month. You'll do O.K., Mike, you're young and talented." Atkins stands up to let Mike know she really does not have anything else to say. What else is there to say? She offers her hand and Mike takes it. He has no bad feelings toward Atkins. She has always been more than fair and besides, it's the economy, it's not her fault.

Good work. Do everything possible to leave on good terms with your employer and co-workers. They are still good contacts and you may need to use them as a reference.

"Keep in touch, Mike, I'll keep my ears open for you."

"Thanks, I would appreciate that," is all Mike can manage as he turns and heads for the door. Things had been going so well. He was getting his feet under him financially, and he had learned an incredible amount in the last couple of months. The Anderson/Carter project was the opportunity of a lifetime for a rookie like him. Now, it was over.

Keep in touch with past employers, and ask them to keep an eye out for you for openings in your field.

Another rejection letter. Mike can't believe how frustrating looking for work is. He has been at it for three months and he has had only one interview. It seems like he has talked to everyone he knows and everyone his friends know, and he has tried to be on the lookout for new people to meet. He's hoping Kelly, who he met at the Volunteer Centre, will come through on her promise to talk to a friend in advertising.

Good for you, Mike, keep talking to people. It will pay off!

At ten to four the phone rings.
"Thursday at 1:30," says a voice on the other end.
"Pardon me?"
"It's Kelly. Thursday at 1:30 is your interview. I talked to my friend and he is looking for someone. I told him you were wonderful and he wants to talk to you."

"Small opportunities are often the beginnings of great achievements."
***Bits & Pieces*, Jan. '90**

"Yes! Kelly, your timing is great. It was just turning into one of those 'what's wrong with me and why does no one want to hire me' days. Thanks, I owe you one—a big one."

Mike is ready for his interview. He knows he has to make the most of it if he's only going to get one interview every three and a half months. Besides, he is good at what he does, isn't he?

Be absolutely certain to check your clothes a day before. You don't want to spend the entire interview worrying about your appearance.

Thursday morning rolls around and Mike is up early. There had been no videos the night before. His sports jacket was freshly cleaned, but as he pulls on the matching pants he notices a mud stain on the left leg. "Oh man, not today." Mike has dress clothes, but not that many, and he certainly does not have a huge selection of things he can wear to this interview. He blots at the stain with a damp cloth and hopes he can dazzle them with his skills alone.

12:30. "Car keys, check. Portfolio, check. Atkins' reference letter, check. Last look in the mirror, I look good, check. Resume, . . . resume, Oh no!" Frantically Mike runs around the apartment searching for the disc his resume was on. Good thing it was updated!

 Yes! Keep your resume current. You never know when you may be asked for a copy. Even if you have a job, it is a good idea to have a copy of your resume circulating.

12:50. Mike runs into the copy shop without putting change in the parking meter. "I'll just be a second," he thinks. He rushes to the back of the shop, checking his watch. "Ten to one, lots of time, I'm still O.K., . . . no I'm not!" Both computers are busy. Mike will have to wait.

The minutes tick away and Mike tries desperately not to panic. It is still only one o'clock. He tries to calm down by thinking of some of the things he wants to be sure to mention in the interview: heading up the Anderson/Carter project, the graphics courses he took in school, the increasing responsibility he had been given in his last job.

1:03. The girl on one of the computers is finishing up and printing. Come on printer!

1:07. "Are you finished?" Mike tries to be polite, but he can't keep the impatience from his voice. The girl just nods, but doesn't hurry up.

1:09. Mike flops into the chair and jams his disk into the computer. Two copies should be good since that is all I have time for anyway, Mike thinks. He makes a mental note not to be quite so disorganized next time.

 **We all make mistakes. The key is to learn from them. It seems you are learning, Mike. Good work!**

1:20. Resumes in hand Mike runs for his car and the parking ticket that is keeping it company. "Oh man." He shakes his head and grabs the ticket off the window.

1:26. Mike makes every green light on the way, skids into the first parking spot he sees, grabs his stuff and sprints for the office door.

1:28. "Hi, I'm Mike Connors. I have a 1:30 appointment with Mr. Clarke." Well, he doesn't sound too breathless. He hopes he looks more composed than he feels.

"Have a seat Mike. I'll let Mr. Clarke know you're here."

"That which does not kill me makes me stronger."

Friedrich Nietzsche

Mike sits down and starts to agonize over the morning. Things had started out so well. He had thought he was so organized and then everything . . .

Relax, you're there. Don't dwell on what went wrong. Just take it from here.

"Hello Mike. I'm Steven Clarke. Glad to meet you." Mike stands up, offers his hand and wishes he had had time to stop in the washroom.

Stop in the washroom prior to your interview to check your appearance. Tell yourself one last time how perfect you are for the position.

"So, Mike," Steven says after settling in and making a few idle comments about the weather and how Mike knows Kelly. "Tell me about yourself."

Here we go, thinks Mike. "Well, I went to school in a small town east of the city and kept pretty busy throughout high school. I played every sport under the sun from hockey, basketball, and volleyball to badminton, soccer and track in the summer."

"Do you still do a lot of sports?"

"Yes, I like to keep active. I play in a basketball league and do a lot of running on my own."

"Really, I do about twelve miles a week. There is a great route not far from here in the river valley. You'll have to try it some time."

"That sounds great. I will!" Score one point for our side. Mike smiles to himself.

Excellent! You started off with personal information, things you are comfortable with, and something you may have in common with someone else! Great technique!

"Anyway, from there I went to college here in the city, and as you see in my resume, . . . Oh, I have an extra copy of my resume with me if you would like." Mike leans across the desk and offers a copy of the document that almost made him late.

"Thanks. I gave my copy to the director of marketing to look at." Steve takes the copy and thumbs through it.

"I majored in marketing and minored in computer graphics, so I have a nice balance of the business and the creative side of the industry. I worked every summer while I was going to school and was lucky enough to get an annual job at Hoode Advertising. I did everything there from graphic layout to brainstorming with clients to decide what advertising they needed. Right after graduation I landed the job at Visions Advertising. So, I haven't worked for a lot of ad companies, but the experience I have is diverse and quite extensive."

"Can you give me specifics about the projects you worked on, Mike?"

I hope you're prepared to give examples without prompting. Remember, not all interviewers are good at their jobs!

"Well, initially I started out simply doing the ad layouts someone else designed for magazines and brochures. Then I graduated to designing some of my own stuff. By the time I left Visions I was handling a major ad campaign. I managed everything from print design to an aggressive radio ad series. It was interesting and challenging. Naturally, the client knew how much money they could spend but that was about it. We had to determine where the money would be best spent, what market they were trying to reach and design visuals and script radio spots. Overall, the client was very pleased. I maintained a tight schedule, meeting all my deadlines, and I came in on budget."

Good example, Mike. You gave a broad range of skills, how you felt about the project, and—most importantly—how the client felt about your work.

"If you had the project to do over again, would you change anything?"

Mike wonders where Mr. Clarke is going with that question, but he is confident in his performance. "No, I don't think I would. It was a very successful campaign for them, and we were all pleased with the results. In fact, I brought along some of the print ads I designed. I can leave my portfolio for you to look through if you would like."

Always bring along relevant material for the job you are applying for: portfolios, photographs, written works, etc.

"Sure, that would be great. I'd like to see what else you've done. Tell me, Mike, working that closely with the client, were there times when you disagreed? How did you handle the situation?"

Looks like we're going to get right into things, Mike thinks. "Hmm, you know, I suppose I was quite lucky. The client and I seemed to hit it off right from the beginning. And we were on the same creative wave length throughout the project, so we didn't ever have a disagreement. Sometimes they wouldn't like a particular detail, so we would discuss it and I would make the changes, or they would see why I did what I did, and agree with it."

"I agree, you were lucky you got along. That certainly doesn't happen all the time. So, what would you do if you found yourself in a situation where you and the client couldn't agree on anything and everything you did they hated?"

Remember, interviewers are people too! Don't be afraid to laugh and enjoy your interview. It will make it more pleasant for both of you.

"*Aargh!* That would be disastrous!" Mike makes a face and laughs. Steve grins, and Mike continues. "No, seriously, it would certainly be awkward, but I think it is important to remember who keeps you in business. A customer has an idea in mind about what they want, and you have to help them fine–tune it. I know I can't take it personally if someone doesn't like all of my ideas."

Good. You let them know that you are flexible and willing to listen to others.

"True, that's an essential attitude to have. Can you describe for me a situation where you were in conflict and had to resolve the issue?"

Mike thinks for a second. "To be perfectly honest, Mr. Clarke, I can't think of a situation at work where I needed to resolve an issue before it got out of hand. But there was a time when I was coaching little league hockey and I had a bit of a run–in with one of the parents. We were on the ice at a practice and he came out of the lobby yelling at me to get over there right that second, in front of all the other parents and the kids. So I skated over and he continued to yell at me and embarrass both of us, as far as I'm concerned. Anyway, the first thing I did was suggest we go into one of the dressing rooms to discuss the situation. I made sure he knew that I thought whatever concern he had was important and I would do my best to resolve it. Well, he calmed down long enough to tell me what he thought and it turned out in the end to simply be a miscommunication. I think if you make people feel their concerns are valid, they relax and you can get to the real problem, which is often simply a communication issue."

 If you can't think of an example from your work–related experience, use your extra–curricular activities.

"Yes, that is definitely a valuable skill. What would you say are your three greatest strengths, Mike?"

 It's more than okay to pause for a few seconds to collect your thoughts during an interview. Better that than saying something you regret.

"Gee . . . that's a tough question. I suppose I would have to say my enthusiasm for the work that I do. I think it's contagious and gets other people excited about a project. My computer skills are a definite asset. I'm also creative and I can put my ideas on paper. Finally, I guess I would have to say I'm very thorough. I'm not afraid to research an idea or project to come up with just the right ad or jingle or whatever." Mike shifts uncomfortably in his chair and absent–mindedly clicks his pen. He is not overly pleased with that answer, never having had to answer that question before.

 You did fine, Mike. You illustrated your strengths with concise examples and took credit for what you are good at. If you feel you haven't given a good answer, move on. You can add something later if you need to.

Steven pauses for a second and scribbles a few notes down on a piece of paper. Mike hates it when they do that. "Mike, we do a lot of television work here, everything from writing to post–production work. What kind of experience would you bring to us?"

You **must** research the company prior to your interview so you are prepared to answer specific questions.

Television! Mike wished Kelly had mentioned that when she told him she had a friend in advertising. "Well, actually, I took several courses in college in post–production editing of commercials, infomercials and that sort of thing. I have always been fascinated by the possibilities of television with respect to advertising, and I think it is important to have knowledge and talent in a number of different media. I'm also enrolled in a night course on writing for television and am really excited about that. I enjoy learning the latest techniques and being able to meet and talk with other people in the industry. I find talking to other advertising and marketing people is pretty much the best way to improve your skills." Good grief, Mike thinks to himself. That was kind of long–winded. At least Clarke is still writing things down, so he can't be too bored.

"Mike, where do you see yourself personally and professionally a year from now, and five years from now?"

It is an excellent idea to continually update your education. It adds to your credentials and shows your willingness to learn.

"That is a tough question. To be perfectly honest with you, Mr. Clarke, I haven't thought about it a lot. I hope to be in a solid company I can contribute to and one that will allow me some growth as well. Personally . . . I am certainly not ready to start a family, but I would like to have a serious relationship." Mike is not sure where that question was going or whether he has even come close to saying what Steven wanted to hear. All he knows is that he desperately hopes Clarke will ask him a question he feels confident with.

"Well. Mike. I think that's probably enough for today. I'm not sure if you were told, but we will be interviewing a few people, and today, although we seemed to go into a bit of overtime, was supposed to be a casual get–to–know–you session."

I must have been interesting enough to keep him here a few extra minutes at least, Mike thought to himself as he stood up. "Thank you very much for taking the time to meet with me, Mr. Clarke. It was very nice to meet you," Mike said as he extended his hand for a parting hand shake.

"It was nice to meet you too, Mike, be sure to say hi to Kelly for me." Steven smiles and opens the door.

"Thanks again," Mike turns and smiles as he leaves the office.

 **Oops, you forgot to find out when a decision would be made. Be sure to find out when you can call; it makes the waiting a little less stressful!**

Five days later the phone rings.

"Hello Mike. It's Steven Clarke calling. I hope I didn't catch you at a bad time."

"Hi, Mr. Clarke, no, I was actually just getting organized to head out to an interview." Mike can feel the nervous tension in his stomach and hopes this is not the 'Thank you for your time, we've found some-one more suitable . . . ' phone call.

 Remember to get positive and negative feedback from the employer no matter which way the decision goes.

"Well, I'm glad I caught you then. Listen Mike, I know this is short notice and we never had a really long chat the other day, but I got a good feeling from you and I'd like to offer you the position. If you're still interested I'd like to welcome you aboard."

"Short notice, this is great notice! I'd love to work with your organization. When should I come in to discuss the details?"

Steven laughs on the other end of the phone. "How's tomorrow morning for you? You don't have another interview scheduled then, do you?"

"No," Mike chuckles. "I'll be there."

 **Congratulations, Mike! You did a great job. You were energetic and enthusiastic throughout, even when you felt less than confident.**

VGM CAREER BOOKS

CAREER DIRECTORIES
Careers Encyclopedia
Dictionary of Occupational Titles
Occupational Outlook Handbook

CAREERS FOR
Animal Lovers
Bookworms
Caring People
Computer Buffs
Crafty People
Culture Lovers
Environmental Types
Fashion Plates
Film Buffs
Foreign Language Aficionados
Good Samaritans
Gourmets
Health Nuts
History Buffs
Kids at Heart
Nature Lovers
Night Owls
Number Crunchers
Plant Lovers
Shutterbugs
Sports Nuts
Travel Buffs
Writers

CAREERS IN
Accounting; Advertising; Business;
Child Care; Communications;
Computers; Education;
Engineering;
the Environment; Finance;
Government; Health Care; High
Tech; International Business;
Journalism; Law; Marketing;
Medicine; Science; Social &
Rehabilitation Services

CAREER PLANNING
Beating Job Burnout
Beginning Entrepreneur
Career Planning & Development for
    College Students &
    Recent Graduates
Career Change
Careers Checklists
College and Career Success for
    Students with Learning Disabilities
Complete Guide to Career Etiquette
Cover Letters They Don't Forget
Dr. Job's Complete Career Guide
Executive Job Search Strategies

Guide to Basic Cover Letter
    Writing
Guide to Basic Résumé Writing
Guide to Internet Job Searching
Guide to Temporary Employment
Job Interviewing for College
    Students
Joyce Lain Kennedy's Career Book
Out of Uniform
Slam Dunk Résumés
The Parent's Crash Course in
    Career Planning: Helping Your
    College Student Succeed

CAREER PORTRAITS
Animals; Cars; Computers;
Electronics; Fashion;
Firefighting; Music; Nursing;
Sports; Teaching; Travel; Writing

GREAT JOBS FOR
Business Majors
Communications Majors
Engineering Majors
English Majors
Foreign Language Majors
History Majors
Psychology Majors

HOW TO
Apply to American Colleges and
    Universities
Approach an Advertising Agency and
    Walk Away with the Job You Want
Be a Super Sitter
Bounce Back Quickly After
    Losing Your Job
Change Your Career
Choose the Right Career
Cómo escribir un currículum vitae
    en inglés que tenga éxito
Find Your New Career Upon
    Retirement
Get & Keep Your First Job
Get Hired Today
Get into the Right Business School
Get into the Right Law School
Get into the Right Medical School
Get People to Do Things Your Way
Have a Winning Job Interview
Hit the Ground Running in Your
    New Job
Hold It All Together When You've
    Lost Your Job
Improve Your Study Skills
Jumpstart a Stalled Career

Land a Better Job
Launch Your Career in TV News
Make the Right Career Moves
Market Your College Degree
Move from College into a
    Secure Job
Negotiate the Raise You Deserve
Prepare Your Curriculum Vitae
Prepare for College
Run Your Own Home Business
Succeed in Advertising When all
    You Have Is Talent
Succeed in College
Succeed in High School
Take Charge of Your Child's Early
    Education
Write a Winning Résumé
Write Successful Cover Letters
Write Term Papers & Reports
Write Your College Application Essay

MADE EASY
Cover Letters
Getting a Raise
Job Hunting
Job Interviews
Résumés

OPPORTUNITIES IN
This extensive series provides
detailed information on nearly 150
individual career fields.

RÉSUMÉS FOR
Advertising Careers
Architecture and Related Careers
Banking and Financial Careers
Business Management Careers
College Students &
    Recent Graduates
Communications Careers
Education Careers
Engineering Careers
Environmental Careers
Ex-Military Personnel
50+ Job Hunters
Government Careers
Health and Medical Careers
High School Graduates
High Tech Careers
Law Careers
Midcareer Job Changes
Re-Entering the Job Market
Sales and Marketing Careers
Scientific and Technical Careers
Social Service Careers
The First-Time Job Hunter

 VGM Career Horizons
a division of *NTC Publishing Group*
4255 West Touhy Avenue
Lincolnwood, Illinois 60646–1975